# mirror moments
## poetry of life

mirror moments

# mirror moments
## poetry of life

shubhshree anand

mirror moments



anand.shubhshree@gmail.com
www.shubhshreeanand.com

ISBN: 9798835828067

Illustrations and design by Shubhshree Anand

First Edition

to the one who pushed me
vanrajsinh gadhavi
you gave life to my dreams
thank you
because you believed in me
even when I didn't


to my father,
rajendra anand
who introduced me to
the world of books and reading,
thank you
because that inspired me
to write one on my own


and to all those who pulled me back
thank you because you made me
a poet

mirror moments

to all the books and their writers who inspired me
and has been an important part of my life,
I genuinely appreciate all your teachings and
lessons.

"The Alchemist" - By Paulo Coelho

"By the River Piedra I sat down and wept" - By
Paulo Coelho

"Who moved my Cheese?" - By Dr. Spencer
Johnson

"Tuesdays with Morrie" - By Mitch Albom

"The Calling" - By Priya Kumar

"I am another you" - By Priya Kumar

"Life's Lessons" - By David Kessler & Elizabeth
Ross

All these above books, writers,
and their lessons became
the mirror moments of my life
that made me realize that I too can achieve my
goals and I did it.

If I can, then I'm very sure, you can too.

so go out there and look for your *mirror moment!*

# contents

shubhshree anand

# falling

mirror moments

meaningless relationships
stressful work life
earning so high
yet enjoying so less
while we are running
life in us is still
in search of *living*

- routine

...& ten reasons to love me
but one reason not to marry

- racism

...& sometimes i wonder
what if
survival and dreams could
walk together

- heaven on earth

all this time
i thought this distance
will drift us away
but it was *you*
who made it possible

- long-distance relationship

was it easy for you to say that
"It wasn't easy"?

- breakup

you gave me your permission
but all i needed was your *support*

- parenting?

...& sometimes i fear that *"I"*
might come between *"US"*

- ego

no matter how hard i try
my smile still cries

- breakup diaries

...& sometimes i just want to share my problems
please don't try to solve it

- free advice

working for something i really don't like
yet wondering why i am not happy?

- stuck in 9 to 5

...& you wanted to be
the reason behind my smile
but never tried to find out
the reason for my tears

- love you to the moon and back?

you are in my present
but i am still in your past

- insecurities

"Leave Me", i never said
"I love You", you never get
"Sorry", i always meant
"Don't leave" i always begged
 but you still left...

- breakup

i will wait
till the end
but only if
you are mine

- conditions apply

...& will you love me
when i don't?

- unrealistic expectations

...& i closed all the doors
so you can't leave me
but you found a window

- escape

why do i always fall for those
who can never be mine?

- one-sided love

...& maybe we are like those parallel lines
never making it to the end

- not made for each other

two egos
one relationship
...& it's obvious who is leading

- me over us

dear lost dreams

every day
every night
when my mind is out of sight
unnecessarily fighting useless fights
hope visits me to say hold on tight
self-doubt
pressure
worry
and stress
almost takes away all my light
still, i *lie* that everything's alright
but seriously when i think about my plight
i wonder what if my *life has taken another flight*

i always end up expecting
a forever from those
who are as fleeting as time

- expectations

...& i wish they would have
celebrated my efforts
not just success

- family & friends

few careless moments
& we missed the flight of
our friendship

- lust is blind too

34

...& i have come a long way
to go back to the same place again

- past

...& my eyes search for you in everyone but
the irony is my heart expects
a different story all the time

- wishful thinking

36

whether it was happy or sad
let's stop living there

- past

you were obedient and
i was rebellious
different yet on the same page
as you didn't rebel and i obeyed that

- and we never made it to the end

you gave me everything
except what i wanted

- respect

wafers

then:
one packet of wafers
three hands
one was mine
two were yours
i cried as
i ate slowly
and you ate most of the wafers

now:
one packet of wafers
both my hands
but this time
i didn't enjoy
eating the whole packet
as it was not shared with you

...& i always took a stand for you
even when you were not standing beside me

- love

...& is marriage a good enough reason
for me to stop loving you?

- the end?

we were just 21 hours away from each other
...& i wonder why it took years for us to be together

- long-distance relationship

43

i loved you so i should have stayed
& fought for you
you loved me too
but you were helpless

- excuses

closure

we got hurt
we broke each other's hearts
but i guess while we were
picking up all those pieces
i happened to take some of yours
you might have taken some of mine
maybe that's why
sometimes i cry when you get hurt
as i still have some broken pieces of yours entangled
with mine
i can't be at peace until
you take those pieces from me
so come back
before it's too late
*again*

...& i go back to those memories
as it is the only place
where we are still together

- our happy place

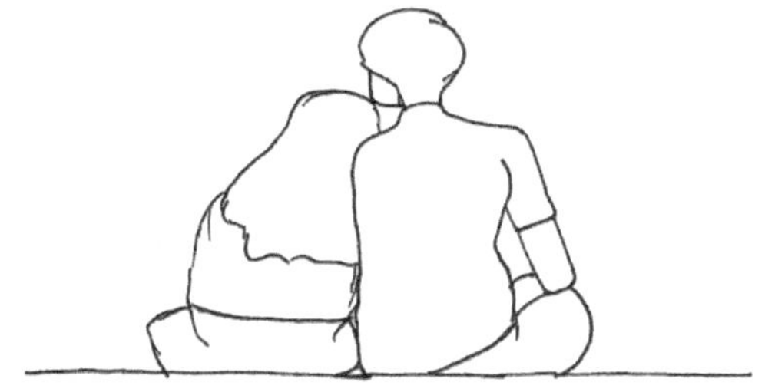

46

you were curious to know
how many times i *slept with* the other guy
but was never concerned
how many nights you made me *cry*

- ex-boyfriend

4-year-old me
14-year-old boy
he touched me and i slept
and i wonder if i was taught the
*difference between*
good touch
and bad touch

- sex education

you prefer to be a secret
while i chose to be an open book...

- opposites attract?

dear ex-boyfriend,

we got into something
we didn't know
and we called it love
without knowing what it meant
but thank god
we did *leave* it
before it forces us
to leave each other
to the one who
made it to the present
thank you for being who you are
or else there would be just a story to tell
not to *live*

*presence*

at first, it delighted me
i forgot every problem
when i was in it
and it became my habit
to stay in it
then i started cherishing it
loving it
and one day
suddenly
i lost it
i cried while craving for it
you told me that my crying
won't make any difference
and after a year
i realized
that i don't want it
because
i already have it
in my smile
in my tears
in our favorite songs
in the innocence of every child
and during all those nights
holding me tight
when i am about to give up the fight

in my mind
in every heartbeat
now i know
i have it
more than ever before
as *your presence*
is present
at the core

# mirror moments

# pulling

# mirror moments

54

my choices were never considered
because even i was busy wearing their shoes

- parenting

...& marriage became
a parameter
to judge
whether it was love or not

- rules of society

they struggled & gave up their dreams for us
expecting the same in return

- parents

in the name of parenting
they made me question
my own dreams

- secured life

i know i mean the world to you
but please give me some space
in your world
to be who i am...

- let me be me

...& they say love can never die
but only If you marry that guy

- beliefs of society

try not to lose yourself
in following the successful crowd

- *be you*

they taught me how to love others
except myself

- upbringing

...& the pressure of being a mediocre
often kills the dreams of creativity

- herd mentality

...& they want their names behind ours
but they hardly stand beside us

- marriage

...& they want me to be like everyone
except myself

- following the rat race

...& they say
money can buy you anything
i always thought
they missed the word
*passion*

- priceless dreams

...& they thought
i was a loser
in a race where
i never belonged

- *rat race*

...& they say
marriage is a compromise
i always thought
they collectively miss the word
*"mutual"*

- rules of marriage

do i need to marry him to be
in love with him?

- boundaries of society

to crave for something, you call a need
doesn't make me characterless

- equality?

...& our parents taught us
the most important thing
about marriage
"never give up"

- marital rape is not a myth

...& i wonder how controlling someone
is parenting these days?

- concerned?

...& we live in a world
where love needs
validation to be true

- love is not an on-off switch

they can gossip
but can't help
they can judge
but can't understand

- best friend forever?

75

*parents* didn't give us the wings
when we wanted to fly
when they gave one
we already made peace with our cage
and that's how they define *freedom*

76

...& we live in a place where
killing is an honor

- honor killing

shubhshree anand

mirror moments

# realizing

mirror moments

when the chaos of life hits you
go out
nature is there to rescue

- find your peace

...& do we have enough time
for the *right time?*

- waiting

83

...& sometimes it's all about
how you end it

- choices that we make

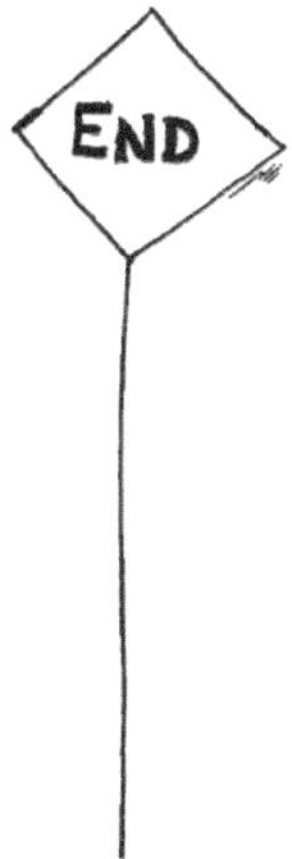

...& how will i find myself
by walking on someone else's path?

- footprints

let's just leave us there
where it was all so beautiful

- our happy place

every path looks good
when you're not sure
about the destination

- career

somewhere between surviving & living
happiness was ignored

- routine life

if you are with the right person
does it matter
in what direction you are heading?

- love

23 years with my parents
yet i can live without them after marriage
6 months of Relationship
& i can't live without you
...& maybe i am not good at calculations

- *love is blind*

somewhere between
"attachment"
and
"feelings"
we misinterpreted love

- friendship

91

i made my own cage of
fears and desires
wishing for freedom

- trapped within

i gave many
second chances
to everyone
except myself

- hypocrisy

winning & losing is just the same,
when you argue with your loved ones

- pointless

having me was neither your good luck
nor losing me was your loss
maybe
it was *just not written*

- destiny

not just relationships
but even a breakup
needs understanding


- the missing piece

...& nowadays
when i see people
i miss something
maybe it's *life*

- mirror

97

if my understanding & love
changes with the relationship
then i am sorry
i bluffed us

- *camouflage*

we fell in love
unaware
of the fact that
we define love differently

- love misunderstood

...& maybe
i'm there beyond those colors
wishing to meet myself
before the sun sets

- self love

in the circle of life
i realized that
it's the *presence*
not presents
that matters

- all we need is time

i carried my baggage of fears
and wondered
why i couldn't do anything in life

- self-doubts

persistence will always disappoint you
in a world
where *change is the only constant*

- ego

do we really have problems or
are we living in the past?

*- understanding*

...& *NO* is a word
we all say
but never listen

- humans

...& my love feels that
there can be only one relationship for us
the one we can't have

- marriage

...& to all the things that ever went wrong,
"you were always right!"

*- perspective*

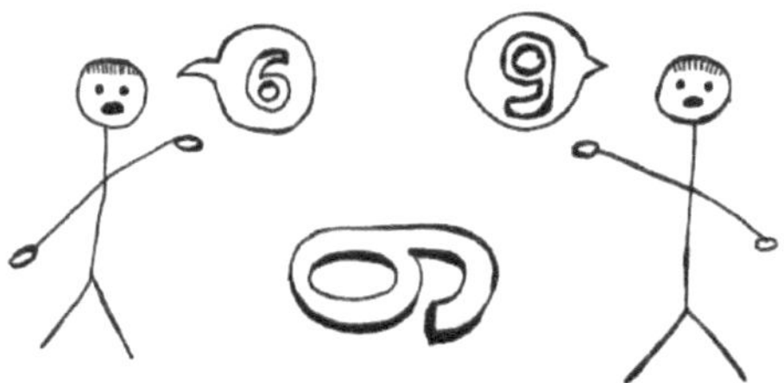

everyone *needs someone*
maybe that is why
we often fall for anyone

- relationship

...& we all are working hard to get a
*fancy cage*

- is this life?

...& somewhere between
"fighting with her"
and
"fighting for her"
we grew up

- *mother*

...& they want to get closer
when it's wet
but don't even care
when it *bleeds*

- periods

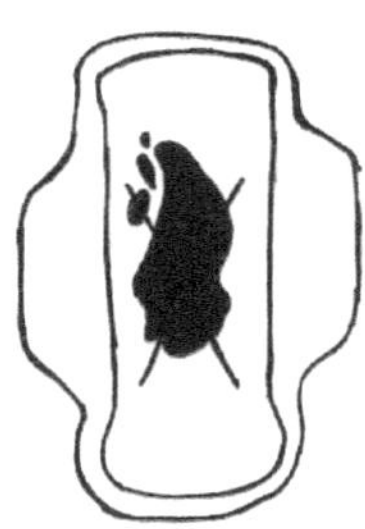

...& they can't eat from their plates
but they can rape

- *untouchability*

...& they demand respect
without giving it

- *men*

words aren't enough
to show your *respect*
you need to have it in your heart

- relations

...& maybe
we are climbing a mountain
by drowning deep in the river

- *education*

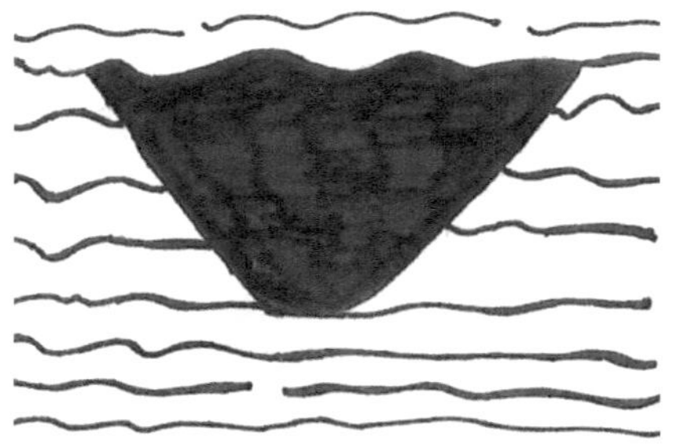

...& in reality
there is no
finish line
so let's just
enjoy the
journey

- *life*

we all are walking on an endless path
yet we are expecting to reach somewhere

- paradox

...& somewhere along the way
the bills due became *larger than our dreams*

- trapped mindset

endless bitching
sharing memes
is that what we call
*friendship* nowadays?

- best friends forever?

shubhshree anand

119

...& we all get *trapped* in
wanting new friends and
needing the old ones

- college to office

...& they belong to two different worlds
i wonder
if a compromise can keep them *together?*

- arranged marriage

after a few years of your marriage
i realized that
i don't need to kiss you
to *love you*

- breakup

if you live *independently*
they all will
blame you
judge you
criticize you
for not sacrificing
*yourself*
to make their house a home

123

...& we all are *finding ourselves* in others
some are *glad* in the end
while some are *blaming* others

- reality

in the chaos of jealousy and insecurities
love took a *backseat*

- love misunderstood

125

...& we need *courage*
not permission to fly high

- dreams

while misunderstanding
and helpless situations
were being blamed
*intentions* got ignored

- broken heart

shubhshree anand

.

mirror moments

# changing

...& i do cherish my memories
but
i have stopped staying there
*forever*

- let it go

did you leave the one who left you?

- breakup

when i lost you
i *found* me

- eureka

...& from loneliness to solitude
eventually
i found my paradise

- *change your perspective*

one day, you doubt me
next day, you trust me
and then you ask me
how can i change?

- *irony*

if you can live *with her* happily
then
i can live *without you*
happily

- unconditional love

137

break the chains
before it breaks you

- cross your boundaries

i never left you
but now i will
before we hurt each other
in the *name of love*

- divorce

...& maybe
we all are of the *same shapes*
just *different sizes*

- humanity

...& what do you think should be new
in a *new beginning*
the surrounding
or you?

- move on

...& someone asked me,
"what made you free?"
i replied, "those who left me"

- speed breaker

...& we have the courage
to start a new life with a new person
but not with *ourselves*

- fill your own cup

...& let's make it simple this time
expect what you can give

- *commitments*

we give all our efforts
to take a perfect picture
then why not our lives?

- social media

moving on

i thought while standing midway
whether to go back or stay
my mind questioned
aren't they both the same way?
staying is going back
to those old days
staying is waiting
with the hope that
everything will again
be the same way
and that was all i used to pray
but deep inside
i know that past is far away
the vague road ahead of me
seems the only ray
of hope
of the new beginnings
of helping me to leave all those memories
and grudges at the bay
i started to walk in that new way
and soon i knew that staying back was making me
the prey
i hope that someday
all this will make sense
when
*moving on*
will surely pave a way

...& then there are a few places
which i *never left*

- childhood

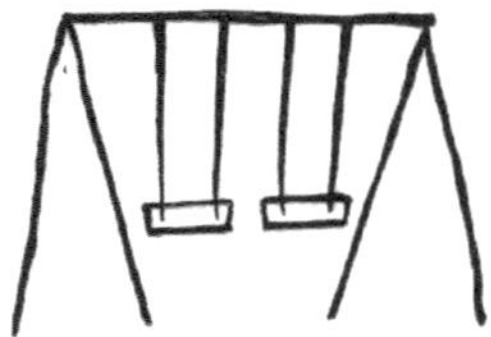

colors
lights
beach
...& do we need anything else
to fall in love?

-nature

148

...& somewhere in the silence
between our conversations
love found the room

- bliss

...& we are about to begin our new journey
where *love will grow with us*

- together we are better

...& with everything else
he gave life to my dreams

- *love*

151

...& somewhere between
holding on
and letting go
i grew up

- life

...& somewhere between
"losing hope on love"
and "finding you"
i finally met the *flawless version of me*

- soulmates

*solitude*

a cup of tea
with fresh air
few stars to accompany
listening to my favorite songs
and that's how i define my *perfect evening*

*the missing piece*

*you*
out of nowhere
entered my life
days passed
months passed
and we became *best friends*
with you, i started smiling
like never before,
because of you
i never felt alone
even when i was lonely
our understanding grew together
it made our lives back to life
you know what
after last time
i was *broken*
used to think a lot before taking
a single step
but now i am willing to take
every risk
for you
for us
after a year
i feel like i have found that *missing piece*
which completes the puzzle of my life

## love will find you

the days when i used to get fright
you were there to hold me tight
never had i thought before i took the flight
that now who will hold me in the lonely nights
i turned every argument into a fight
but you were the one who was taking it so light
you are my sunshine so bright
my glowing moon in the night
i think that is why i feel so alright
because no matter wherever i am
you are always in my sight
no matter whatever be the plight
i know you won't leave me
while others might
our love has reached that height
those three words have importance so slight
with you
everything feels so right
my search for true love came to twilight

# mirror moments

# growing

don't give up on your dreams
just because you aren't sure of the end

- *keep walking*

take a moment to stop
and enjoy where you are
before you reach your destination

- *enjoy the journey*

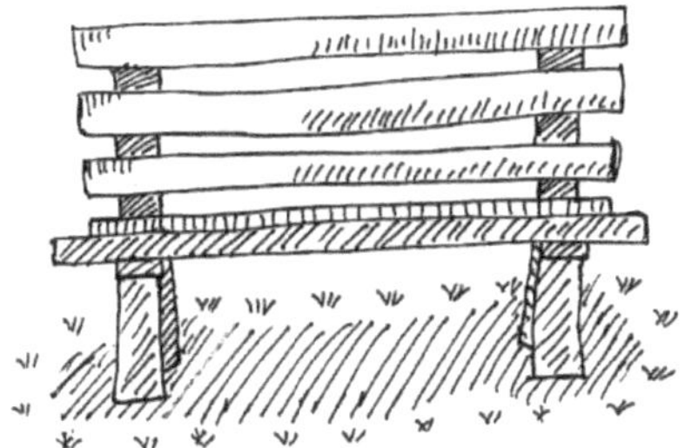

what we are focusing on
is always our *choice*

- perspective

...& it's okay to *choose*
different directions

- break the pattern

don't lose your *self-respect*
in the name of love

- rose tainted glasses

mirror moments

164

your happiness is what matters the most
even though if it's with someone else

- *unconditional love*

it's a mixture of everything
and that's what makes it so
beautiful

- *life*

*dreams* are the price
we pay for our survival

- choice

no matter how comfortable you might be
a cage is always a cage

- set yourself free

...& after all the hustle of life
i realized that
i already had everything
i ever wanted

- it's all within

why use labels?
they are just words
and who needs words
when you have feelings

- relationship

are we in love with the companion?
or the surroundings?

*- love misinterpreted*

understand
that not everyone can
understand you

- expectations

172

choose them and you don't have self-respect
choose yourself and you are selfish

- choice

shubhshree anand

friendship
relationship
marriage
you gave importance to these *labels*
while i just gave it to you

- and all this time i thought we were in love

2 boyfriends
1 fling,
and that's how they define
*"characterless"*

- and that's how society thinks

175

and take a walk with nature
you will end up finding yourself

- peace

if we can start with friendship
why can't we end it with that?

- *choices*

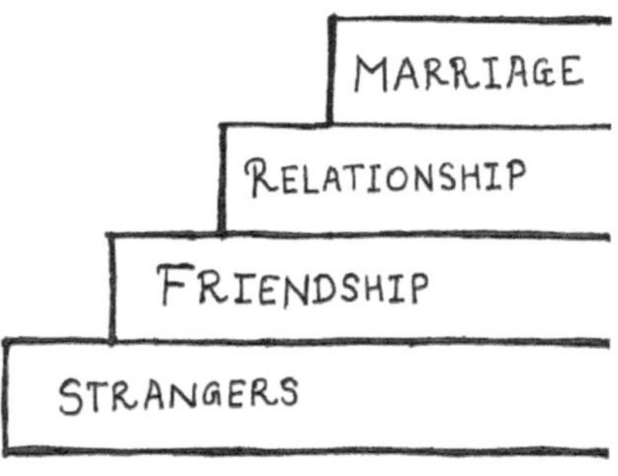

and take a walk into your childhood
to realize that a *happy,*
a *carefree* version of you exists

- look within

dear _______

i don't know
what future holds for us
if there will be a time for us
will it be forever
but i know one thing
that we have this present
this moment
in our hands
as we have this time
to grow together
to live
to make memories
which will last forever
i know i have us
i don't know whether
i will be your
friend
girlfriend
wife
but i know
one thing for sure
whatever i will be in future
i will always be there for you

179

can we once walk on the path?
without the expectation to reach
our desired destination?

- idealism

water it as much as you can
not in the greed for the fruit
but just for its *growth*

- relations

...& why do we wait for dates to change in order to change?

*- slipping moments*

obsession
insecurity
possessiveness
the modern words for *love*

- millennials

...& i wonder how being afraid of losing someone
is called love these days?

- insecurities

...& somewhere between "appreciating his work"
and "working for his appreciation"
we grew up

- *father*

## remember it's just a device

we met
we sat
we talked
for a while
about our
careers
and relationships
until your phone
beeped
which took more than
a minute
maybe
just a minute
no big deal right
and we lost the track of
our conversation
with that interruption
so what
we can always start over
right
and yet it happened
again
then again
it seems the phone
connects
everyone better
than they can
and just before i wanted to tell you
something
the time smiled

as our interrupting conversation is
about to end
and before we left
i told you to put your phone
next time on
*silent*
so that we can break the
*silence*
between us

next time
let's just put our
phones aside
and express the depths of our hearts
which can't be
expressed by the emojis
let's just look into one's eyes
without taking it off
or sticking it onto some device
maybe we forgot
it's just a *device*
which helps us to connect
when
we are far
but it's making
us fall apart
so just one question before i leave
that phone is with you all the time
but what about us
are we guaranteed the next time?

shubhshree anand

*can we stop
running?*


there is a racetrack
with no finish line
and
we all are in that race
trying to reach the end
copying everyone we see around us
especially those who think they are
about to reach the finish line
and following them blindly
never wondering what if
we all have different races
so reaching the finish line of those
we follow blindly
won't lead us
where we actually meant to
we don't even realize to stop before
we reach somewhere we don't even know

*let's leave this stupid race*
ask yourself
do you really want to win?
do you really want to play that game?
where one thing is guaranteed

that you will lose
because you are in the wrong place

*can we stop for a moment?*
let's stop
let's breathe
and savor
the moment
the journey
the different paths
let's find what's meant
for you on your path
you see
individuality is just not about our
name
skin
sex
family
caste
or religion

it is also about
our
dreams
and
purpose of our life
*let's find ourselves*
and who knows
we might find our purposes on the way

my heart fell for you
but you left me
without a word
and showed me the
*mirror*
that I
deserved
someone
better

- myself

*Shubhshree Anand*
-    A little girl with not-so-little dreams

once upon a time
in the fall of '94
a girl was born
who happened to be shy
started her journey reading books
observed people and their lives
and began imitating them
first by joining the rat race in school
working hard to be a topper in the class
further followed what the crowd was chasing

started reading fiction
and self-help books
which made her wiser
at a very young age
she was a reader before
she became a writer
not to forget the detour of 6 years
where she pursued engineering

a broken heart can either
make you
or break you
the choice is always yours
and that's what happened with her
a breakup that made her a writer

shubhshree anand


her pain became a stepping stone
which led her to poetry
and she believes that every failure is a lesson
for years she kept writing what she felt
and then she wrote a poem about the rat race,
which showed her the mirror
and she penned down her first book,
"mirror moments".


-    about author

mirror moments
is a collection of
*poetry* about
the phases of life
such as
falling
pulling
realizing
changing
growing
which will help you
in finding solutions to
the unresolved problems of your life

mirror moments is a book
full of uncertainties
just like *life*
which will help you in
enriching your understanding of life
finding yourself
forgiving your past
and self-love

and somewhere along the way
you will find yourself and your story in this book

-   about the book

# Connect With Me!

You can connect with me on the following platforms:

 twitter.com/anandshubhshree

 www.shubhshreeanand.com

 facebook.com/shubhshreewrites

 shubhshree.anand21@gmail.com

 medium.com/@shubhshreeanand21

 youtube.com/shubhshreeanand

 instagram.com/shubhshree_anand